The Shortest Stories

The Shortest Stories

A MIDWIFE WRITES BIRTH HAIKU
ON EACH BEGINNING

Janelle Alier

GOOD PRINTED THINGS

Edited by Beth Brown Ables
Cover Art by Kimberly Obee
Book Design by Lib Ramos

First Edition

Printed in the United States of America
goodprintedthings.com
Greenville, South Carolina

ISBN: 979-8-9921993-2-1

The poems contained in this collection reflect the
author's own personal recollections of experiences.
Some names and characteristics have been changed
to protect and respect the privacy of all involved.

This project is funded in part by the South Carolina
Arts Commission which receives support from the
National Endowment for the Arts.

This project is also funded in part by a generous
award from the John and Susan Bennett Memorial
Arts Fund of The Coastal Community Foundation
of South Carolina.

For the midwives and healers in my lineage

—J.A.

RECORDS

Harper 44	*Mav* 46
Henry 47	*Milo* 40
Howie 29	*Noah* 57
Imogen 3	*Nora* 34
James 22	*Oak* 13
Jaxon 41	*Olivia* 37
Jonah 26	*Pearl* 32
Joseph 14	*Peyton* 42
Josephine 39	*Remi* 45
Jubilee 21	*Sadie* 33
Juno 16	*Sage* 31
Kasey 8	*Truett* 25
Levi 30	*Uriah* 15
Mabel 19	*Violet Grace* 48
Magnolia 60	*Willow* 9
Marguerite 26	*Wolf* 59
Mateo 1	

I started writing haiku regularly as a graduate student. My midwifery program had a tradition: the faculty gave each of us a pair of tiny maroon-and-white Philadelphia University socks to gift to the first babies we caught. Instead of sharing a proper clinical account with my classmates and professors, I wrote a haiku to announce the first baby received into my hands as a student midwife.

It's another girl!
Today, I gave away socks.
Thank you, dear Mother.

Perhaps it was just a clever attempt at getting out of telling a long story, but when a classmate responded in kind, the practice took off amongst our cohort. Our program director even read many of our best haiku at our graduation dinner, crediting me with initiating a new tradition. That bit of recognition made me feel special and empowered, like I was onto something that many could appreciate, participate in, and enjoy. In the years after completing my degree, I continued intermittently writing haiku, but it wasn't until I launched my own private practice that I set a goal of writing one for each birth.

Inexhaustibly
excited about my work—
how could I not be!

The truth is, I'm not really a writer or poet. I just happen to have an insanely cool job. Often these verses write themselves. I've learned many things about haiku along the way...including that I write them all wrong! While I follow the 5/7/5 recipe, I do a lot of telling instead of showing. I do not favor

nouns and verbs over adjectives and
adverbs. Proper haiku have no titles, but
I'll never give up lovingly naming them
after the newborns who inspire them.
Fortunately, most midwives are good at
challenging norms and breaking rules!

I find it very hard to write haiku when
I'm trying very hard to write haiku.
The goal of expressing more than seems
possible in just 17 syllables is achieved
when the poems flow effortlessly,
inspired by a vivid experience of the
present moment. Birth is mysterious,
both universal and unique. It can never
be fully explained or understood, but
we always want to try. Writing haiku
has become an important part of my
trying, and I look forward to composing
these short poems as I process and
honor each New Beginning.

Attend your first birth.
You'll want to write a novel,
but you'll be speechless.

I've long cherished the quiet, personal process of reflection and until now, have rarely shared these poems with anyone. I have wanted to be mindful, making sure my own perceptions do not overshadow stories that do not belong to me, but rather to the mothers and families.

Every birth presents profound moments, all experienced differently by the person actually giving birth, than by those bearing witness. Even so, haiku is intended to be shared, often even written collaboratively. This collection, while it may not be that of a haiku master, honors the art form just by its existence. I am so grateful for the thoughtful guidance of my publisher, Lib Ramos of Good Printed Things, and editor, Beth Brown Ables, who have championed this idea into the book you now hold in your hands.

These poems are about bellies, birth, boobs, and babies. Some are humorous, some heartbreaking. Some will make you wonder, and others are universally relatable. Whatever experience of birth you bring with you while reading, I hope this collection of haiku gifts you both inspiration and delight.

Here, in a handful of syllables, we bear witness.

— Janelle Alier

Mateo

Practice centering
radical humility—
Midwife, heal thyself.

Clark

Birth, you Son of a
Car in the road on fire
in the pouring rain!

Imogen

New Year's babe, after
the waters opened last year.
Cheers to beginnings!

Adelaide

She made her own rules.
One minute before midnight,
she met her own goal.

Archie

Fully surrendered,
open hands and open heart,
fully supported.

Arthur

There was no amount
of counter-pressure that could
ever be enough!

Alaia

Here's to the woman
with everything against her—
Now pop the champagne!

Björn

It's a boy! A son!
Received by this mother, then
shared with his father.

Harlow

Progress is possible.
Eat, drink, soak, rest, push, pull, curse.
It's not guaranteed.

Anya

Psychosomatic,
lack of shared reality—
groomed in Jesus' name.

Kasey

X-ray of the soul—
an inconclusive report.
Remove with a knife.

Willow

If you're still singing
about a magic Journey
we know you're not close.

Finley

Labor Yelp review:
One star, do not recommend,
very bad service!

Duncan

Plumbing Cervices:
Unclogged in just 4 minutes!
A 5-star review.

Ember

Pandemic Mother—
dumpster fire survival.
What will happen next?

Oak

Pandemic midwife—
still counting births while the world
was counting the deaths.

Felix

Pandemic baby—
the world is in need of you,
a wise and old soul.

Arden

Oh my god, I thought.
How is this something that's real?
Whose idea was this!

Joseph

Rallying after
a crisis of confidence—
a superpower.

Uriah

Quick, just like we thought.
I left footprints through the dew
as I ran inside.

Juno

Giving birth alone—
my love letter to nature,
signed, sealed, delivered.

In February
I buried her placenta
under red callas.

Emma Dale

A full moon, blood moon,
A seventh child, daughter,
born with the lightning.

Fiona Jean

Number one hundred—
home birth under a full moon,
hand-picked from the stars.

Adelynn

The badass in me
salutes the badass in you.
That's it. That's the poem.

Mabel

I'm good at the job—
a force to be reckoned with.
I'm only human.

Banner

3-year-old in tears—
the baby didn't say "Hi!"
Crushed expectations.

Jubilee

"I don't think mom knew
the baby would come tonight!"
—awakened Big Sis

James

Am I living right?
Is some star in retrograde?
Asking for a friend.

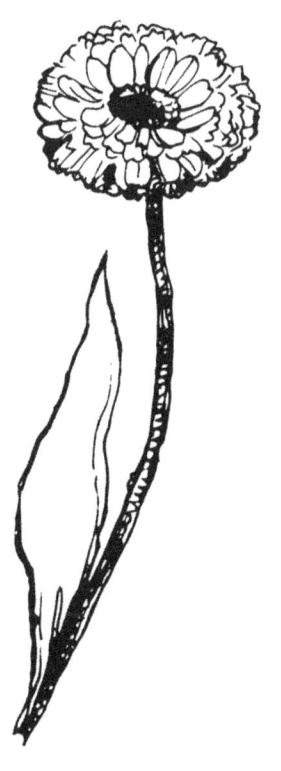

Truett

Next time ask sooner.

"Humor me with just one squat?"

One was all it took.

Jonah

She birthed in sunshine,
while a wren worked on her nest
outside the window.

Marguerite

I tried to advise
extra rest- sit on your nest-
anodyne wisdom.

Freyja

Two baby chicks hatched
the same morning I was gone
catching a hatchling.

Calla

"Maybe you should swear,"
says my favorite doula.
"Cussing always helps."

Howie

"I was not myself!
Sorry for what I said when
I was in labor."

Levi

This is L&D?

Where people come to give birth?

No one knows what's up!

Sage

Sometimes there are themes.
Violet, Lily, Oak, Willow—
Botanical names.

Pearl

Bright morning in May—
"I've never had one outside!"
A seaside homebirth.

Sadie

I don't think I can—
a truly tender sentence.
Then we always do.

Nora

Weary and doubtful,
but like a band of rebels
we white-knuckled faith.

Olivia

A cesarean
even after everything
done well and right— rude!

Ellis

She wanted homebirth.
She can't control the weather—
refugee at Mom's.

Adler

Hurricane Helene—
gusts of wind and sheets of rain
brought her labor pain.

Josephine

I really don't mind
blood and fluids on my shoes—
but they were brand new.

Milo

Birth ephemera—
affirmations on the wall,
the twinkle lights hung.

Eleri

The Pink Pony Club
Galentine's slumber party,
open five hours.

Jaxon

I knew it was on
when I saw her typically
perfect hair a mess.

Lost in labor land,
coaxed out from under the porch
like a mother cat.

Peyton

Hypnobabies says
you get the pain you expect.
Sometimes you get more.

Elouise

Maybe it's worth it
to take a chance with Christmas.
There is more magic!

Harper

Babies are like fruit.
Good things, that fall from the tree
only when ready.

Anndee

Sunday morning births
have always been my favorite—
the world in stillness.

Remi

Birth follows no rules.
Control is an illusion.
Mystery abounds.

Mav

Savoring what was
while grieving what wasn't is
beautiful tension.

Henry

Valor: Bravery,
especially in battle.
Scars tell one story.

Violet Grace

Birth ripped my heart out.
There is no good reason why,
but I still want one.

Banks

"It's time to give birth."
A little pep talk gave a
lot of permission.

Dietrich

I didn't mean to
hurt the baby Dragonfly.
It was a mistake!

Cecelia

The maiden has died,
reborn anew as Mother—
Divinely painful.

Esther

A Benediction—
This is my body, broken
for you. Come. Take. Eat.

Colette

Pregnant at Advent,
I went to the midnight mass.
Mary, pray for me!

I'd rather be flung
into oncoming traffic.
I said what I said.

Hot white pain, vomit,
primal mammal animal,
tears, blood, and curse words.

Harlan

"If this isn't real,
Mother Nature is a bitch!"
[birth]
"That wasn't so bad."

Evie

"Dang it! Have mercy!"
Five minutes later, sister.
"Wow, that was something."

Noah

Negotiations,
patience, and intercession—
Promises made good.

Cadon Joy

Are there no limits
on the tragedy and hurt
one mother must hold?

How could she not act?
Anger, my lazy response,
comes so easily.

Wolf

Mother so peaceful,
midwife hyper-vigilant,
Wolf cub at midnight.

Daniel

Miracle Baby—
said about all, true for some.
It is true of you.

Magnolia

The wisdom and proofs
of those who have gone before
will carry you on.

Bella

Center gratitude.

Focus on your own deep work.

Drink your tea slowly.

Janelle Alier is a Certified Nurse Midwife, devoted to supporting women and families through all stages of pregnancy, birth, postpartum, and beyond. Originally from the Midwest, Janelle has lived and worked in Greenville, South Carolina, for more than twenty years. She believes in the importance of informed choices, partnering with expectant parents, and encouraging them to make their own best decisions for health and well-being.

Graduating from Philadelphia University with a Master's degree in midwifery, Janelle has honed her skills in both hospital and community settings. Most recently, Janelle opened her own private practice in 2019, Paris Mountain Midwifery, named after a beautiful local landmark, where she resides with her family.

Good Printed Things is a small press located in Greenville, South Carolina.

Our projects facilitate collaboration between writers, designers, and artists, and showcase the good that comes from these intersections of talent.

Each printed thing we make reminds us of the value of tangibility in an increasingly digital world.

goodprintedthings.com

www.ingramcontent.com/pod-product-compliance
Lightning Source LLC
Chambersburg PA
CBHW051643120626
46551CB00015B/2202